Unicycle Dad

BY **SARAH HOVORKA**

ILLUSTRATED BY **ALICIA SCHWAB**

TO MY DAD, FOR SHOWING ME HOW TO SUCCEED.—S.H.
FOR MY BROTHER, TOBIN.—A.S.

Text copyright © 2024 Sarah Hovorka
Illustrations copyright © 2024 Alicia Schwab

Published in 2024 by Amicus Ink,
an imprint of Amicus
P.O. Box 227, Mankato, MN 56002
www.amicuspublishing.us

Library of Congress Cataloging-in-Publication Data
Names: Hovorka, Sarah, author. | Schwab, Alicia, illustrator.
Title: Unicycle dad / by Sarah Hovorka ; illustrated by Alicia Schwab.
Description: Mankato, Minnesota : Amicus Ink, [2024] | Audience: Ages 5–9.
| Audience: Grades K–1. | Summary: Sarah compares her family's life with
a single father to riding a unicycle, a balancing act that is sometimes
difficult but also filled with joy and love.
Identifiers: LCCN 2023018970 (print) | LCCN 2023018971 (ebook) | ISBN
9781681529028 (hardcover) | ISBN 9781681529035 (pdf)
Subjects: CYAC: Family life—Fiction. | Single-parent families—Fiction. |
Parent and child—Fiction. | LCGFT: Picture books.
Classification: LCC PZ7.1.H6818 Un 2024 (print) | LCC PZ7.1.H6818 (ebook)
| DDC [E]—dc23
LC record available at https://lccn.loc.gov/2023018970
LC ebook record available at https://lccn.loc.gov/2023018971

Designed by Lori Bye
Edited by Rebecca Glaser

First edition 9 8 7 6 5 4 3 2 1

Printed in China

Unicycle
Dad

BY SARAH HOVORKA

ILLUSTRATED BY ALICIA SCHWAB

amicus
INK
MANKATO, MINNESOTA

Whoosh!

When Dad first starts pedaling, the unicycle pitches forward and the wheel slides backward—whoops!—until he gets going and za-za-zooms up and down our street like a flying bird.

I want to soar like that, too.

When I try, I just wobble—PLOP!
Dad pulls me to my feet.
"It only takes perseverance, Sarah.
Keep trying until you get it."

He makes it sound easy.

Slowly . . . Woah!—and carefully—phew! No way I'm letting go of the wall! The ground looks so far away.

Too soon, Dad says, "Time to start dinner." He doesn't have anyone to help since Mom left. He does everything—even his job as a janitor and going to school—by himself. He's all alone. A uni-parent.

"Spaghetti again?"

"It's what we can afford.
But I'm graduating tonight! Then I
can get a promotion at work."

As we get ready, Dad says, "This graduation won't be as grand as a high school graduation." He goes to continuation school. It's for people who didn't have the chance to go to regular high school.

I say, "I'm going to finish high school right away. And I'm going to college."

At the ceremony, my brother, John, and I are as proud as can be.

After Dad gets his diploma everyone clap! clap! claps! and cheer! cheer! cheers! The principal says a whole lot about how my dad is hard-working and he'll soon soar to great heights.

But Dad doesn't get a promotion.
Instead, he has to get a second job
at night, and we get a babysitter.

Most days I practice on the unicycle and
do my homework, but it doesn't feel like
soaring. It feels like hard work. Some days
I want to give up.

I keep trying, though, just like Dad does. To help him out,
I teach myself to cook.

"This doesn't taste like Dad's spaghetti," John complains.

"That's because it's Big Sis spaghetti, with my secret
sauce," I tell him. "I worked hard on it."

John works hard, too.

For John and me, the days feel loooooong
without Dad around. Sometimes I wonder if
I'll ever see Dad ride the unicycle again.

One evening—BAM!—the door swings open. "Dad, why are you home so early? Is something wrong?"

Then I see the laugh in Dad's eyes. It spills right out of him and rushes over me. "I did it! I got the promotion!"

My heart leaps. My feet follow. "Hooray!"
I ask, "Does this mean you'll be home more?"
"Yes, and I can't wait to spend more time with you both.
You guys are the reason I worked so hard and never gave up.
And I noticed all your hard work, too, my two high-flyers."

He wraps his arms around us (squeeze) and starts to
spin around. I laugh as I rise like a sailing kite.
"How should we celebrate?" Dad asks.
"Ice cream!" John yells.
"Yes! Let's ride there!" I say.

"I don't know if I can pedal the whole way there," John says.

I smile at him. "It only takes perseverance," I say.

Dad laughs as he hops onto the unicycle.

After a pitch forward and a slide backward
he gets going and za-za-zooms ahead.
Someday, I'll soar like that, too.
But for now . . .

Whoosh!

The Real Unicycle Dad

Unicycle Dad is a true story from my childhood. Here we are!
We were a small family, but we knew how to be strong.

I still remember my dad's graduation. Today, he's at the top of his career: Director of the entire department!

As for me, I have my own family now. And we're never too far from the real Unicycle Dad.

P.S. I never learned to ride the unicycle, but I had another dream to be a writer. And with that, I found my own way to soar.